THIS IS ME!

THOUGHTS OF YOUNG POETS

Edited By Sarah Waterhouse

First published in Great Britain in 2023 by:

Young Writers® Est. 1991

Young Writers
Remus House
Coltsfoot Drive
Peterborough
PE2 9BF
Telephone: 01733 890066
Website: www.youngwriters.co.uk

All Rights Reserved
Book Design by Ashley Janson
© Copyright Contributors 2023
Softback ISBN 978-1-83565-217-6

Printed and bound in the UK by BookPrintingUK
Website: www.bookprintinguk.com
YB0572U

FOREWORD

For Young Writers' latest competition This Is Me, we asked primary school pupils to look inside themselves, to think about what makes them unique, and then write a poem about it! They rose to the challenge magnificently and the result is this fantastic collection of poems in a variety of poetic styles.

Here at Young Writers our aim is to encourage creativity in children and to inspire a love of the written word, so it's great to get such an amazing response, with some absolutely fantastic poems. It's important for children to focus on and celebrate themselves and this competition allowed them to write freely and honestly, celebrating what makes them great, expressing their hopes and fears, or simply writing about their favourite things. This Is Me gave them the power of words. The result is a collection of inspirational and moving poems that also showcase their creativity and writing ability.

I'd like to congratulate all the young poets in this anthology, I hope this inspires them to continue with their creative writing.

CONTENTS

Drongan Primary School, Ayr

Gracie Clarke (9)	1
Star Crainie (10)	2
Star Johnston (9)	4
Mia-Belle Linwood (9)	6
Adam Harper (10)	7
Lyle Armstrong (10)	8
Lucas McCutcheon (10)	10
Kennidi McCafferty (10)	11
Mason Hogg (10)	12
Riley Smith (10)	13
Isla Brown (9)	14
Jack Renwick	15
Kendal McCulloch (10)	16
Kyira McCulloch (10)	17
Elise Ferguson (9)	18
Ollie McKinlay (10)	19
Ryan Kelly (10)	20
Lexie Stark (10)	21
Riley Campbell (10)	22
Blayre Miller (10)	23
Kyle Lees (9)	24
Ella Gemmell (10)	25
Daniel Patrick (10)	26
Ava Agnew (10)	27
Rocco Little (10)	28
Harry Dunlop	29
Lilly Mitchell (9)	30
Kari-Rose Cowan (10)	31
Aila McCutcheon (10)	32
Murray McAdam (9)	33
Kerr Young (10)	34
Scott Lindsay (10)	35
Alexander Johnston (10)	36
Hollie Hughes (9)	37
Kayla Dewar (10)	38

Gawsworth Primary School, Gawsworth

Marlee Few (7)	39
Fearne Parker (8)	40
George Marsden (7)	41
Lottie Davis (7)	42
Skyla Houghton (7)	43
Harry Austin (8)	44
James Tandy (7)	45
Jayden Francis Martinez (7)	46
Alannah Corr (7)	47
Eden Ball (8)	48
Hector Stallard (7)	49
Freddie Petrie (7)	50
Pheebie-Rose Devenport-Barsted (7)	51
Reuben Hassall (7)	52
Eliza Bradley (7)	53
Reuben Cairns (7)	54
Anya McMurdo (7)	55
Henry Bell (7)	56
Aeson Sumner (8)	57
Sennen Few (7)	58
Olivia Horn (8)	59

St Mary's Catholic Primary School, Loughborough

Keiran Comodero (11)	60
Alana Whiteman (10)	67
Victoria Gladiseva (11)	68
Nayara Gondar Aboo (10)	70

Willington School, Wimbledon

Sophia Woodward (7)	71
Saam Bemana (10)	72
William Draper (8)	74
Amelia Li (7)	75
Edward Robinson (10)	76
George Tasev (7)	77
Ayshani Duwadi (8)	78
Dohyeon Park (7)	79
Jack Cormack (10)	80
Sebastian Dickens	81
Sotirios Xathakos (10)	82
Flynn O'Hara Thomas (10)	83
Jasper Woodward (9)	84
Leo Andarias Yip (9)	85
Mark Perry (10)	86
George Cant (10)	87
Nicholas Tan (8)	88
Amber Kim (7)	89
Amrit Cheema (9)	90
Bode Hills (9)	91
Hunter McCrossen (11)	92
Charlie Nailon (10)	93
Violeta Perez Lopez (7)	94
Thomas Maddison (10)	95
Rory Bush (7)	96
James Douglas (10)	97
Tom Parry (7)	98
Ian Byun (9)	99
Oscar Ahmadi (10)	100
Eshan Sujenthiran (7)	101
William Campbell (10)	102
Samuel Reeve (9)	103
James Lloyd (9)	104
Alex Bartocci (10)	105
Hudson Walker (9)	106
Felix Bown (9)	107
Elias Carle-Edgar (10)	108
Danny Han (7)	109
Perry Davis (9)	110
Raphael Balthasar (7)	111
Samuel Cryer (10)	112
Charlie Laffey (9)	113
Jack Gale (9)	114
Edgar Favre (9)	115
Joseph Benjamin (9)	116
Amy Choi (7)	117
Aaron Li (9)	118
Alexander Harvie (9)	119
Benji Hutton (10)	120
George Hanna (7)	121
Aemelia Flook (7)	122
Eddie Rossmann	123
Adam Radwan (10)	124
Christian Stephenson (8)	125
Seojun Kim (10)	126
Heather Maddison (7)	127
Gio Lee (7)	128
Alfie Danson (7)	129
Oscar Caceres (7)	130
Noah Kingsley-Benjamin (10)	131
Sonny Browne (10)	132
Alfie Harper (7)	133
Calum Stimpson (7)	134
Jasper Cristina (8)	135
Ayoon Jeong (7)	136
Vasil Vasilev	137
Joe Blythe (7)	138
Luca Broere (11)	139
Julian Paul (7)	140

THE POEMS

This Is Me

You will need:
1 cup of laughter,
3 bottles of height,
£10 of a pet owner
9 cubes of age
12 spoons of kindness
9 cups of purple dye,
Lots of family and friends and
Lots of glitter

Method:
Now you need to add friendliness and a cup of laughter till warm
Next, add three bottles of height because I'm as tall as a giraffe.
Now add £10 of a pet owner
Get another bowl and mix 9 cubes of age and 12 spoons of kindness.
Pour it in the other bowl.
Add 9 cups of purple dye, my favourite colour.
Finally, add family and friends.
Bake to finish with a sprinkle of glitter.

Gracie Clarke (9)
Drongan Primary School, Ayr

To Make Me, You'll Need

1 tablespoon of height,
3 pots of mood
2 spoons of black,
300lbs of music
1 teaspoon of reading,
20 cups of laziness,
1 pint of love,
10 buckets of boredom,
50 spoons of being strange,
1 pinch of talent,
1 dash of fun,
7,000 cups of games
1,800 pints of radness,
1 spoon of weirdness.

Now mix 10 bucks of boredom together with 7,000 cups of games
After firmly mixing for five minutes
Add 300lbs of music and let it sit for one hour.
After an hour, add in 1 pint of talent and 4 dashes of fun
Stir for ten seconds

1,800 pints of radness
Finally, put in the oven for thirty minutes
Then, add 1 spoon of height
3 pots of mood
50 spoons of being strange
1 pint of love
1 teaspoon of reading and
29 spoons of laziness!
Now you have me!

Star Crainie (10)
Drongan Primary School, Ayr

All About Me

As grateful as a frog
But also kind.
Cats like to lick me.
Dogs like to play with me.
Ellie is my favourite name.
Frogs are my favourite animal.
Goats make me laugh.
Horses make me happy.
I love eating apples.
Jam is my papa's favourite thing.
I always kiss my nan on the cheek at bedtime.
Lions are loving to me.
Monkeys make me giggle sometimes.
My nan is loving to me.
The ocean makes me happy and peaceful.
Primary, 6 is my year.
Writing is fun.
The stars in the sky are peaceful.
Tea is my favourite thing to drink.
Violins are what I play with.
I'm only allowed to drink water in bed.

I used to play with yo-yos.
Zebras make me giggle too.

Star Johnston (9)
Drongan Primary School, Ayr

About Me!

To create me, you would need:
A kingpin PE lesson.
10lbs of art supplies.
1 gallon of helpfulness.
5 whole buckets of family and friends.
A couple of teaspoons of blush-pink and sky-blue.
A couple of pieces of jewellery.
Some spoons of brown hair.
My dogs, Roxi, Drake and Lady.
A few teaspoons of Nike clothes

Now you need to:
Stir it hard until it's softer,
Add a few sprinkles of glamour
While stirring softly, spread it onto a tray of cupcake moulds and put it in the oven for 10-15 minutes and then leave to cool.

Mia-Belle Linwood (9)
Drongan Primary School, Ayr

Want A Chat?

Hi to the person who is reading this,
I'm going to tell you all about me.
So, what is your favourite thing in the world?
It could be a person, place or an animal
I will give you time to think
Ohh, interesting!
Me, personally,
I love my grandpa because he makes me laugh
and he even made me a treehouse with my uncle.
So, what are your favourite hobbies?
Mine would be football.
I am a determined defender
What are your favourite hobbies...?
Ohh, interesting!
Bye-bye!

Adam Harper (10)
Drongan Primary School, Ayr

This Is Lyle

I'm normally grumpy,
Really gummy.
I have gherkin eyes,
And I like pies.

I hate eagles,
But I like beagles.
I like to play football,
And I'm tall.

I have football skills,
To pay the bills.
I don't like big cranes,
But I have a good brain.

I heard a creak,
But I fell asleep.
I fell on my arm,
I fell on hay in a farm.

I'm not a bit apprehensive,
But I'm appreciative.
I kicked it an angle,
But it started to tangle.

Lyle Armstrong (10)
Drongan Primary School, Ayr

About Me

T he energetic and very enthusiastic person I am.
H i, my name is Lucas, I am in Primary Six, also I am calm.
I am helpful, also an animal lover, also have syrup-brown hair, love bears.
S ee me, you will see syrup-brown freckles, also caramel-brown eyes.

I love doing maths and writing in school, also art and football.
S ee me eating chicken nuggets and pizza.

M y favourite colour is sapphire-blue and honey-yellow.
E veryone plays football at school.

Lucas McCutcheon (10)
Drongan Primary School, Ayr

This Is Kennidi

T all in size,
H elpful to other people, even strangers.
I love my family and friends with all my heart.
S chool has my favourite subjects, art and PE, they will always be my favourites.

I n PE, we're doing King Pin and it's my favourite game.
S ometimes, I can be energetic, just not in the morning.

M y favourite colours are lavender-purple and pink.
E ven football is my favourite, jewellery, dogs and food are too!

Kennidi McCafferty (10)
Drongan Primary School, Ayr

Read About Me

I love to eat food,
Because I think it's good!
I love to laugh,
And do maths!

Callum Beatty is my favourite singer,
And the sore bit of a bee is its stinger.
I play football because I live,
And I'm very competitive!

I am the best at maths,
But PE is still class!
I may be young,
But I have a long tongue.

I'm always helpful,
And try to be cheerful!
I'm very giggly,
And very clumsy!

Mason Hogg (10)
Drongan Primary School, Ayr

This Is Me

T he summer is my favourite because it's sunny for me to play football.
H ardworking during school time.
I 'm a speedy superstar at football.
S trawberries are my favourite fruit to eat

I have dark brown eyes and hair.
S uper football player

M y favourite position is midfield because I'm a marvellous midfielder
E ating McDonald's is my favourite thing to do.

Riley Smith (10)
Drongan Primary School, Ayr

About Me

I like art and playing parts in assemblies.
I like flowers and flowing in the wind
I am brave and going into a cave
I like chocolate and choco.

I am good at football and hurting my foot
I am calm when I see a lamb
I am when I am being perfect.
I like books and cookers

I have fire hair, fire blood
I am a baker who likes to bake
I like dogs and gods
I am short and portable.

Isla Brown (9)
Drongan Primary School, Ayr

This Is Me

A spoonful of shyness,
No drops of anger,
A pinch of silliness,
A drop of funniness,
A splash of green,
A teaspoon of happiness,
2 grams of chat,
A cup of brightness
A gram of generousness
A teaspoon of mathematics,
A cup of letters,
A drop of speediness,
A cup of hyperness,
A jug of basketball,
A blob of artiness,
This is me.

Jack Renwick
Drongan Primary School, Ayr

About Me

T hat was a very kind kid.
H orse riding is my favourite hobby!
I 'm in love with Nike clothes and shoes.
S ometimes, I'm lazy or energetic.

I have brunette-coloured hair.
S unflowers are one of my favourite flowers.

M ost of the time, I wear jewellery.
E nergetic I am, well, that's what I'm told.

Kendal McCulloch (10)
Drongan Primary School, Ayr

This Is Me!

I'm as brave as a lion,
As fast as a tiger,
Sneakier than a snake,
As funny as a monkey,
I can be brave when swimming
I can be confident when helping out
Knowing if I do something wrong,
I can fix it.
I'm as tall as a giraffe
My eyes are bluer than the sea,
My friends are short and tall
They are also really funny and kind.

This is me!

Kyira McCulloch (10)
Drongan Primary School, Ayr

My Recipe Poem

To create me, you will need
1 spoonful of fun
2 spoonfuls of prettiness
3 cups of height
1 bottle of kindness
A dash of cuteness
5 cups of good drawer
20 cups of dog lover
10 teaspoons of blue colouring
A dash of excitement
2 cups of happiness
2 bags of friendliness
10 bags of family
Mix this all together to make me!

Elise Ferguson (9)
Drongan Primary School, Ayr

This Is Ollie

T he thing I am good at is maths.
H arry is my friend.
I gloos are very cool.
S teak is one of my favourite foods.

I am always hungry.
S uárez, Messi and Neymar are the best trio in football history.

M onkeys are very cool and funny.
E va is my big sister.

Ollie McKinlay (10)
Drongan Primary School, Ayr

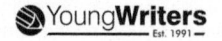

This Is Me

T V to watch Man City games.
H aaland's skills are as good as mine.
I like to ride my bike.
S uperman is my favourite superhero.

I like chocolate ice cream
S nakes are my second favourite animal

M y rabbit is my favourite animal.
E mily is a cheeky monkey.

Ryan Kelly (10)
Drongan Primary School, Ayr

This Is Me!

  L ove my family
  E mbrace my life
e **X** cellent at reading
  I am as cool as snow
  E normous heart

  S oup is my fave food,
  T ry new things all the time!
  A mazing at most things!
  R eally try to improve my writing!
  K ind to others.

This is me!

Lexie Stark (10)
Drongan Primary School, Ayr

This Is Me!

T he football is good to watch or play
H ome, the place I like to be
I watch the games with Dad
S houting and cheering when goals are scored

I am as goofy as a baby
S uper tidy boy

M any games of football I go to
E njoying watching people score goals.

Riley Campbell (10)
Drongan Primary School, Ayr

How To Create Me

10 animal lovers
100 lazinesses
200 talking Irishes
5 TikToks
3 cups of boredom
6 cups of football
7 cups of kindness
5 cups of maths
6 cups of lovingness
400 cups of dumbness
8 cups of music
2 cups of oddness
9 cups of healthies
10 cups of watermelon
500 cups of figure skating.

Blayre Miller (10)
Drongan Primary School, Ayr

This Is Me

T he thing I am good at is writing
H arry is my best friend
I am tired and hungry
S nakes are my third favourite animal

I like KFC
S ometimes, I play with my dog

M y hair is ginger and I have blue eyes
E ven I can't hold my breath for one minute.

Kyle Lees (9)
Drongan Primary School, Ayr

This Is Me!

To create me, you will need,
A soft blanket-filled room,
A bowl of kindness,
A teaspoon of mischief,
A 100lbs of craziness,
1,000 cups of dog lover,
2,000 teaspoons of a mum's girl
20,000lbs of family lover
A teaspoon of annoying trouble,
A teaspoon of teal food colouring,

This is me!

Ella Gemmell (10)
Drongan Primary School, Ayr

This Is Me

To create me, you will need
A dash of honesty
A sprinkle of happiness
5,000lbs of craziness and pizza
A pinch of brightness

Now you need to:

Add 5,000lbs of craziness and pizza
Mix it in, then you need to
Add the dash of honesty and pinch of brightness
Then, cook it for twenty minutes.

Daniel Patrick (10)
Drongan Primary School, Ayr

All About Me

    T all I am and brave.
    H ave liked horse riding.
    I am calm and like dogs.
    S o, fave colours are blue, purple.

    I love PE and Nike.
    S o, I like food and drink.

I' M long and cheerful.
    E lephants are my second favourite animal.

Ava Agnew (10)
Drongan Primary School, Ayr

How To Make Me

T ea with three sweeteners and lots of milk.
H am sandwich with butter
I like to play VR.
S ometimes, I pet my dog, Bear.

I invite my friends to my house.
S eeing my cousins.

M y PS5 I like to play
E njoying PE at school.

Rocco Little (10)
Drongan Primary School, Ayr

This Is Harry

T he thing I am good at is eating
H arry is very grumpy and tired
I love my dog, Hugo
S occer is my favourite

I am talented
S ometimes, I am very clumsy

M essi is the best football player ever
E ating is my favourite.

Harry Dunlop
Drongan Primary School, Ayr

This Is Me

I am an animal lover.
I have a dog called Maggie.
I am creative
I am as brave as a lion.
I am as kind as a doctor and a nurse.
My hair colour is brown with blonde bits through it.
My eyes are as blue as the ocean.
I am a horse rider.
I love horses.
This is me.

Lilly Mitchell (9)
Drongan Primary School, Ayr

The Heart In Me

3 cups of laziness.
4 cups of kindness
6 cups of animal lover
1 cup of oddness
2 cups of music
7 cups of talent
10 tablespoons of generosity
5 teaspoons of ruby-red, cyan
7 pints of gaming
21 tablespoons of moodiness and strangeness
3 teaspoons of love.

Kari-Rose Cowan (10)
Drongan Primary School, Ayr

This Is Me!

I am as brave as a lion,

I am as fast as a time Machine,

I am a superstar writer,
I am as jumpy as a monkey,

I laugh like a hyena,

My eyes are as blue as the Atlantic Ocean,

My heart is as big as the Earth.

Aila McCutcheon (10)
Drongan Primary School, Ayr

This Is Me

He is a young boy in a
Family.

He has short blonde hair and
Has a cute cat with brown
Fur.

His cat is a female and
Likes playing with toys for
Cats.

He likes sport and is a
Sporty child sometimes.

Murray McAdam (9)
Drongan Primary School, Ayr

This Is Me

I have two cats that are the same colour,
I have a turtle that has a really colourful tank,

I have an Xbox and Nintendo Switch
I have a quad and an E-Bike,

I have a triple bunkbed,
I have really good Pokémon cards.

Kerr Young (10)
Drongan Primary School, Ayr

This, Me

T raining for football all day
H i, my name is Scott.
I like to play my Xbox.
S ee my friends, to play outside

M y friend is called Jack
E njoying playing football with my friends.

Scott Lindsay (10)
Drongan Primary School, Ayr

This Is Me

I'm very happy and very funny
And I'm tall and I have lots of friends,
I love maths,
I am really good at it and my favourite thing to play is
Football, and Roblox,
I am very nice too.

Alexander Johnston (10)
Drongan Primary School, Ayr

This Is Me

T iny in size.
H yper!
I love family.
S hy!

I love school.
S assy!

M aking new friends.
E lephants are fun animals.

Hollie Hughes (9)
Drongan Primary School, Ayr

This Is Me

I am a
Superstar defender
Chocolate eater
Book reader
Football watcher
Speedy defender
Early riser
Light sleeper
Rugby watcher
And finally
A good helper!

Kayla Dewar (10)
Drongan Primary School, Ayr

Me And My Family

I am an artist
I love cats and
I go to swimming and
I hate the ancient Romans.
I eat calamari in restaurants and
It is yummy and crispy.
I have a cat and
I have lots of Lego
When I say lots, I mean lots
I like ancient Egypt.
I am a twin, but most importantly,
I am me.

Marlee Few (7)
Gawsworth Primary School, Gawsworth

The Musical Cat

There is a cat, a musical cat
There is a cat, a musical cat
There is a cat, a musical cat
A music cat
What would you get as a musical cat?
Music is everywhere I go
I am a loud and a brave musical cat
I am the musical cat
This is me.

Fearne Parker (8)
Gawsworth Primary School, Gawsworth

The Running Footballer

I love football,
I'm in midfield.
I pass and dribble
I shoot and score.
I'm fast and strong.
No one passes me.
My team is Tytherington Juniors
We're unstoppable.
This is me.

George Marsden (7)
Gawsworth Primary School, Gawsworth

I Like To...

I like to eat.
I like to dance.
I like to sing
And that is what I do.
This is me.
Last of all, I
Drum roll, please
I like friendship.
This is me!
I like to cuddle Mummy and Daddy!

Lottie Davis (7)
Gawsworth Primary School, Gawsworth

The Musical Dog

The musical dog
The musical dog
He's so cute
I don't know why but he is a musical dog
Musical dog
Why won't you buy him?
He is a musical dog!
This is me.

Skyla Houghton (7)
Gawsworth Primary School, Gawsworth

Untitled

I am Harry
I am cool and love school
I am Harry
I love topics, especially the tropics
I am Harry
I love tag with my friends
I don't always win when I get to the bin.

Harry Austin (8)
Gawsworth Primary School, Gawsworth

Me And My Bear Bear

I love my Bear Bear
Yes I do.
I love my cat, Simba
Yes, I do.
I love to give him a belly scratch.
Yes, I do.
They make me feel happy.

This is me.

James Tandy (7)
Gawsworth Primary School, Gawsworth

The Anonymous Boy

I hold meetings,
I investigate the
Imposter.
I like to be turquoise
I have a little dog
He solves the crimes
With me.
I eat pizza
While I play.

Jayden Francis Martinez (7)
Gawsworth Primary School, Gawsworth

My Kitten Pumpkin

I love my pumpkin, yes, I do
He's fluffy, sweet and cuddly too
He had three brothers and sisters with a mummy
But I am his mum now, yippee!
This is me.

Alannah Corr (7)
Gawsworth Primary School, Gawsworth

Me, Plain Me

I am a roast dinner lover,
Gravy is the best.
Running is my sport
The wind in my hair.
Tea and pizza are the best.
I love my family
This is me.

Eden Ball (8)
Gawsworth Primary School, Gawsworth

Drawing Gamer

I like drawing comics.
I am a gamer.
Minecraft's for me!
I have my own character, Dino-man.
Whoopee!
I am kind and caring.
This is me!

Hector Stallard (7)
Gawsworth Primary School, Gawsworth

Me

Pigeons scare me,
But I like rats.
Football is my game,
But acrobatics is not.
I put out fires on BBQs
With my water gun
This is me.

Freddie Petrie (7)
Gawsworth Primary School, Gawsworth

Just Me

I like myself
I am smart
I am beautiful
I can do it
I can do anything
I am glittery
I am funny
I am Pheebie.

Pheebie-Rose Devenport-Barsted (7)
Gawsworth Primary School, Gawsworth

Roblox Max

I'm a gamer
I play Roblox
I'm still learning
I'm a survivor
I've got through all levels
This is me.

Reuben Hassall (7)
Gawsworth Primary School, Gawsworth

Go-Karts Go

Go-karts, go with me
Mummy goes slow and
Daddy goes as fast as can be
Freya goes slow and fast
So do I
This is me.

Eliza Bradley (7)
Gawsworth Primary School, Gawsworth

Me

I am smart, I am cool
I am funny, I'm smart
In Lego, I'm chilled
I love Christmas and my birthday
I am Reuben.

Reuben Cairns (7)
Gawsworth Primary School, Gawsworth

Anya And Her Life

I am Anya, my eyes are blue.
I love my cats, do you?
I like to play as well.
I like grapes, I'll eat them every day.

Anya McMurdo (7)
Gawsworth Primary School, Gawsworth

Me And My Prime

I'm a Prime lover
I could eat seafood every day.
I'm an animal lover and a sporty player
Real Madrid is my team.

Henry Bell (7)
Gawsworth Primary School, Gawsworth

Me And My Sports

Football is fun
Tennis is terrific
Rugby is rough and
Lacrosse is not lame
Sport is my game
This is me.

Aeson Sumner (8)
Gawsworth Primary School, Gawsworth

All About Me

Hi, I am Sennen
I love pizza and games
And I love Xbox
This is me
Sennen.

Sennen Few (7)
Gawsworth Primary School, Gawsworth

This Is Me

I am perfect the way
I am
And I am beautiful the way
I am
This is me.

Olivia Horn (8)
Gawsworth Primary School, Gawsworth

The Epic Of Kieran

In a mysterious realm,
Where courage met fate's decree,
Kieran had a heart,
Who was pretty eager to meet someone,
His mind is sparkling like the stars,
His eyes were wild like the ocean,
His body was thick just like a curvy, reddish tomato.

Days after days, weeks after weeks,
Kieran would still not find a rival,
He was not even interested in a battle,
Months and many months passed by as Kieran came along the long, sweaty desert.
Sand was flowing relentlessly,
There was a boy who was standing ponderously,
Waiting for him to say a word, or so on.

The boy who was standing was something of a mysterious kid,
Starting sternly at him with no expression,
He had a sarcastic ironic smile,

"Well... what do we have here?"
He asked with a devilish grin,
He looked both sides and he rolled his eyes,
Kieran looked at the mysterious boy and then he blurted out,
"I was here because I was there for a rival."
With those words, the boy did one step closer and he was breathing roughly and then stopped,
"What aspect of rival... mate?" he asked him in a wonderful tone.

The wind was rushing fast and the sand flowed beneath their feet,
The boy coughed softly as Kieran said this,
"For fighting."
Kieran was looking at the boy in a focused, roguish mood that expressed that he was even concentrated,
The boy laughed mournfully and sulkily,
As he took off his mask,
"My name's Ario..."
Keiran was looking at him in confusion,
"What? Are you my friend at my sc... c... ch... school?" he stuttered in an unamused mood.

"No... I'm not your friend.
I've never heard of your 'school' and your friends."
He smirked and stared at him,
He looked like he was sarcastically staring at his own soul,
"Well, who are you then?!" shouted Kieran,
"I'm Ario Izurio..."
He looked at Kieran with a serious look in his eye.
"Well..." Kieran coughed, softly again,
"Well, you want me to start the fight?" Ario Izurio said, angrily,
"Uhh... Yes!" Kieran looked at him in confusion and surprise
But he had a feeling that he had to concentrate all over again.
"Heh... Let's see if you can do this..."

As Ario Izurio had a mischievous smile,
He started running at Kieran with a distant rate
But he failed like a coward, trying to aim at something,
While Kieran began to dodge Ario's attacks and tricks
He began using his dark power of all time

Ario Izurio had been tricked by his dark power of all time
However, Ario Izurio dodged the dark power and smirked at Kieran.
"Heh... Oh, Kieran... You think I w-"
Ario Izurio got interrupted by Ario Rizi (the real Ario)
And also Leo, who were riding on horses.

Ario and Leo looked at Kieran in a disappointed way
As Ario and Leo dropped off on their horses,
They walked up to Kieran and then looked at Kieran in a serious way.
"Where's our money?"
Kieran was confused and replied, *"Uhmmmmm."*
As Ario Rizi and Leo looked at Ario Izurio,
Leo looked at Ario Rizi and then turned back to Ario Izurio,
"You must be one of the Iranian gangsters out here...
Are you? Ario Izurio?!"
Leo looked at Ario Izurio in a serious mood,
Raising his eyebrows.

The wind rushed through as Ario and Leo looked together in disbelief
As they looked like they were disgusted,
The clouds shape-shifted like devastation,
And it was evening,
Ario Izurio stomped as the wind got relentlessly stronger,
Stronger, stronger and stronger while Kieran began to use invisibility,
Ario and Leo did not know what to do,
But they looked at their horses and saw their horses were gone;
However, the sand got ultra thick and started to form a sand tornado.

Kieran, with invisibility, walked slowly and crept slowly like a mouse
Swish... Swash... Swish... Swash... went Kieran stepping in the sand,
Ario Rizi had no idea but got a tennis gun
But this was not what he had expected, seriously,
"Grrnnhhh!"
He looked at Leo in an angry mood,
"Leo! Give me a real gun!"

Ario got angrier than before,
Looking at Ario with a bad look,
"Ario! I do not have one!
Not even one or two..."
Ario had a new idea as he liked to think of something else,
The wind got stronger and then stronger
But Kieran decided to stop the fake Ario (Ario Izurio) by distracting him.

As Leo and Ario searched everything in their bag
Ding! Bang! Kwash! Swish! Bonk! Crraasshh!
"Oh, hey, Ario! Look, a tennis gun!"
Ario Rizi pointed at Ario Izurio like a sniper.

When Ario Rizi shot the tennis ball from his tennis gun at Ario Izurio
Poof!
Kieran turned off his invisibility
(Like a light flickering)
Poof!
Ario Izurio flew off to space like an asteroid, flying
Ario did not know what was going on,
So he did not notice that Hades was watching them,

In an unknown manner, Ario Rizi, Leo and Kieran noticed a red portal was coming
And as Hades walked past through the portal gates,
He looked at them in a sternly-mattered way.

Keiran Comodero (11)
St Mary's Catholic Primary School, Loughborough

Secrets

This is me.
Yes, I have all the tea.
If you shout my name, I'll come in one, two, three.
I know I'm loyal,
Secrets can get told
Because I'm too old.
You can trust me if I like you.
Sometimes, I can see through you.
If you see me eating lunch, then come to me
And spill your tea.
I'm always free.
If you know me,
Secrets can be dangerous, especially with me.
I've had years of being clueless to secrets throughout my life,
So, all I'm saying is, don't tell secrets,
I'll always come in one, two, three.

Alana Whiteman (10)
St Mary's Catholic Primary School, Loughborough

My Alphabet

As my alarm rings,
I start off my day,
And my favourite things,
Wake me up all the way,

I could tell you the alphabet,
Of all my most-favoured things,
But this one you will not forget,
Believe me, it clings,

I've got amphibians, bowling,
Cinema too.
Dogs, earrings, fencing,
Gum and haikus!

Islands, jewellery,
Kiwi, luxury,
Music, notebook, ocean,
Don't forget peach!

Quails and rice,
Salami,
Ukelele, voyages,
TV!

Xylography,
Yoga (we can't miss that out),
Zombies, to be honest,
A menace to start.

That is my alphabet,
It really is!
Hope you have had fun with me,
Well, that was a whizz!

Victoria Gladiseva (11)
St Mary's Catholic Primary School, Loughborough

The World's Colours By Feeling

My life is green,
Sometimes blue,
I see colours as emotions,
That change through life too.

My life is mostly green,
Sometimes red,
And too many emotions,
Fill up my head.

My life is sometimes green,
Then my head fills up with the colour brown,
And I don't do anything,
Until the day something comes round.

Nayara Gondar Aboo (10)
St Mary's Catholic Primary School, Loughborough

Sophia's Cook Recipe

1 litre of happy mood,
3 teaspoons of magical dust,
Sprinkle a few pieces of book corner chunks,
1 teeny tiny piece of angriness,
10 chunks of loveliness,
And 11 pieces of love,
10 huge bowls of animal love.

Put it in the oven for 8 minutes only,
Take it out and give it a blow,
You should see it bubbled up,
Now pop all the bubbles,
Cut it in the middle,
You can see now it is rainbow with colours of emotions,
You probably know by now, if you don't know - it's just all of the rainbow colours,
Slice it for you,
If it's good, you can share,
If it's not, don't say, "Don't eat it!" to your friends and family, they might like it,
That's my recipe.

Sophia Woodward (7)
Willington School, Wimbledon

On The Field, Where Dreams Unfold

In the park, with friends so fine,
We play a game, it's football time!
Kicking the ball, with all our might,
Under the sun, from morning till night.

The goalposts set, at either end,
We chase the ball, my best friend.
Running fast, our hearts a-pumpin',
With every goal, our spirits jumpin'!

We cheer and shout when we succeed,
Celebrating every goal we feed.
With muddy knees and messy hair,
We play the game, we are quite a pair!

Our crimson red kit, bold and bright,
On the field it is quite a sight.
In every match, it stands out strong,
As we play all day long.

The final whistle, it is time to go,
But we will be back, this much we know
Football's our passion, it is clear to see,
The game we love, my friends and me!

Saam Bemana (10)
Willington School, Wimbledon

I Am Happy

H ope is good and it can make me happy.
A pples are my favourite fruit, when they crunch it makes me smile.
P urple is the colour of happiness, like a ripe plum on a tree, it makes my eyes happy.
P laying Lego Mario with my sister is always fun.
I ce cream piled high with chocolate chips makes me happy.
N ovember is the month before Christmas, fireworks light up the sky, I love the blue ones that go across the sky.
E aster is fun and full of joyful egg hunts, my tummy is happy.
S ummer is the most fun, hottest, happiest time of the year, water fights, barbecues and holidays are fun.
S afe in my bed, reading Beano or Bunny vs Monkey, I am happy now.

William Draper (8)
Willington School, Wimbledon

This Is Amelia

A iden is my little brother and my best friend
M y favourite sports are swimming and netball
E very day, I go to school
L ook, my friend and I are playing football at the field
I have a little brother
A pple is my favourite fruit.

A n ice cream makes me happy in summer
M y favourite ice cream is chocolate ice cream
E very day, I dream about wintertime
L ots of snow can make me a big ice cream
I love building a snow panda in winter
A snow panda is made of snow and chocolate, yummy!

Amelia Li (7)
Willington School, Wimbledon

The Greatest Showboy

Hi... my name is Ed
I'm always tired because I never go to bed
I don't like broccoli, I don't like mathematics
I really like sport. Good job I'm not asthmatic
I love, love cricket cause I'm a spin bowler
And when I play football, I always think I'm Zola
I also like Chelsea with manager Pocchetino
I love reading comics, especially the Beano
I like to sing, especially in a choir
We're learning how to sing Handel's Messiah
Come and see me at Saint John's Smith Square
Or at the Oval, you'll see me there!

Edward Robinson (10)
Willington School, Wimbledon

George

A pple, I like to nibble
L ots of friends I have
L eo is my football mate

A ce in football, I like to be
B eing a good friend is important
O nions make me cry
U nfair games too
T igers are my favourite animal

G ems are the treasure I have
E nergy I have to play
O range is the taste I like
R ats are the animals I despise
G uitar is the instrument I play
E pic fights I like to watch.

George Tasev (7)
Willington School, Wimbledon

All About Me

B FFs
E very girl is the best
A lways be kind
U nicorns are the best
T he best princess ever
I love Black Widow
F ully rainbow
U nicorns are the best
L ove bunnies and cats.

I want to be an artist,
I love sweets and McDonald's,
I love acting and movies,
I have a big brother, he is 11,
I absolutely love tacos and pizza,
My hair is black,
My eyes are brown,
Last of all... I love poetry!

Ayshani Duwadi (8)
Willington School, Wimbledon

All About Me

I am a YouTuber,
I have 21 subscribers,
I play football and shoot like a football player,
I always want to be a cuber,
I am faster than light,
And I can do running at night,
I am good at everything that we use,
But I want to be a football player and that is my goal,
I like to bake and especially cake,
I like to look at small flags that are under my leg,
I don't like a fight,
I like yellow sunset lights,
But I don't like black nights.

Dohyeon Park (7)
Willington School, Wimbledon

Jack

J ack is the name, dancing round is the game
A ll the while not taking the blame
C heeky child, though
K ind and mild

C ool cats make me happy
O scar, my brother, smells like a nappy
R eading and eating delicious food
M aking Lego puts me in a happy mood
A n architect is what I want to be when I grow up
C reating buildings and skyscrapers whilst
K icking a football to win a cup.

Jack Cormack (10)
Willington School, Wimbledon

This Is Sebastian

I am as cheeky as a monkey, and I enjoy riding my bike
But I really don't like going on a hike
I am quite smart, and I love creating art
I am always very happy, and sometimes a little too chatty
Football is my favourite sport, and I love to build fantastic forts
One of my hobbies is playing a Nintendo Switch game, and I also have a big brain
I like making music at home with my drum kit
And I really, really want a sand pit.

Sebastian Dickens
Willington School, Wimbledon

The Me Rap

FadeTech is my call,
I like to play football,
I'm a wall in rugby,
Nobody can size me!

5' 3" in the back,
No slack!
Got a problem,
I'm good at solvin'
I ain't mean,
I am a goal machine,
Wins I got,
I get them a lot!

No one, no one,
Tall enough
To see my wide grin!
No one, no one
Fast enough
To see me racing up the stream!

Sotirios Xathakos (10)
Willington School, Wimbledon

A Droplet Of Water

D ripping down, making a gentle splash, splosh.
R oaring couldn't be so different to the many droplets swirling in one spot.
O vals running down the edge of the fall.
P lenty of droplets, there is no stop. Pitter patter, pitter patter.
L et us go see the graceful droplets with glee.
E ating and drinking; they're not so different.
T hirst is the ultimate test of the drips and the drops.

Flynn O'Hara Thomas (10)
Willington School, Wimbledon

A Recipe For Disaster

First, gather loads of chocolate and a lot of Lucozade
Stir in some of your scrumptious chocolate and some delightful marshmallows
Season with some ice cream and bravery and sweets
Add a pinch of cheekiness
Pour in a bomb of adventure
And a sea full of Lucozade
Blend in the good times with the bad times to create many movies and childhood memories

Then, gently pour in a sea of love and family.

Jasper Woodward (9)
Willington School, Wimbledon

My Recipe Poem For Leo

First, gather dogs and sport
Stir in my dog's big, comfy bed and a teaspoon of fluorescent cereal
Season with big, dusty books and a splash of energy
Add a pinch of adventure
Pour in a mountain of love and animals
Mix in thousands of gallons of history and music
Blend in building, eating, sleeping and sweets
Warm gently by going on a long, tiring walk and cuddle down peacefully after.

Leo Andarias Yip (9)
Willington School, Wimbledon

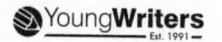

The Witching Hour

When I was four, the night was dreary and I kept hearing the creaking of the floorboards,
My brother snoring loudly like a pig
All these things prevented me from my sleep.
I waited and waited, the clock was clicking
Tick, tock, tick, tock
Until I heard footsteps,
The suspense was killing me
Until my dad's head peeked round the corner and said,
"Wake up!"

Mark Perry (10)
Willington School, Wimbledon

Great Oak, Great Oak

Great oak, great oak, share your wisdom please,
For you have experienced the world from just a tiny seed.
You have the eye of an eagle, yet your roots dwell,
Beneath the earth itself.
Your bushy leaves change colour every day,
Green with pink,
Verdant green,
Crispy brown,
And then, none to see.

Great oak, great oak, towering so high,
What treasures did you conceal?

George Cant (10)
Willington School, Wimbledon

This Is Amazing Me

N icholas is my name
I like puffing puffins that are not the same
C hinese and Malaysian are my relatives
H ot after doing exhausting exercise
O ften I don't like replies
L ove maths and geography
A ge of mine changes slowly as a snail
S andy beaches are one of my favourite places

T ons of knowledge as this is me!

Nicholas Tan (8)
Willington School, Wimbledon

My Favourite Animal

My favourite animal has four legs,
It has soft fur,
It catches mice,
An owner cares for the animal,
They sometimes scratch people,
It has small ears on the top of its head,
It licks its fur,
It is scared of dogs,
It says meow,
It likes its owner,
It is cute and sometimes mad,
It is small and when it grows up, it is going to be big,
It is a kitten.

Amber Kim (7)
Willington School, Wimbledon

What I Love In A Great Recipe!

First, gather fearsome tigers and juicy lemonade
Stir in a jug of kindness and bravery
Season with lovely games and enjoyable sports
Add a pinch of adventurous friends
Pour in a mountain's worth of honesty
And tubs of magnificent, boiling books
Blend intelligence and athletism and wrestling and cycling
Then, warm gently by calculating mathematical equations.

Amrit Cheema (9)
Willington School, Wimbledon

A World I Can Live In

First, gather FIFA and roasting my sister
Now stir in beating Perry in football, plus drinking Orangina
Season with fun and stealing
Add a pinch of evil and sleeping
Pour in making James look dumb while crashing into a chum
And eating, plus being dim while throwing a bin
Blend good-looking with fat
Then, warm gently with joyfulness, oh what it is like to be me.

Bode Hills (9)
Willington School, Wimbledon

Happiness

H appiness is the way to go
A lways stay happy and never be sad
P lay with happiness in your mind
P ositivity is the best thing to think about
I n any dark times, stay happy
N ever give up on your dreams
E very time you feel upset, look forward to better times
S tay strong in mind
S eek joy every day.

Hunter McCrossen (11)
Willington School, Wimbledon

Dogs

The cutest of creatures
With their wagging tails
They come in all different shapes and sizes
There is the Labrador
Of great size and strength
There is the chihuahua
With a big sense of ferocity for something so small
There is a daschund
With a long body of a sausage

They come in all different sizes, but they are all special to me.

Charlie Nailon (10)
Willington School, Wimbledon

Me!

V iolet is the colour of my name
I love books and picking flowers
O range juice is yummy, especially if my mummy makes it
L earning history and geography is so much fun!
E lephants and zebras are among my favourite animals
T ravelling lets me discover amazing places
A nd learn interesting things about them.

Violeta Perez Lopez (7)
Willington School, Wimbledon

Thomas, This Is Me

T homas is my name, being terrific is my game,
H orses are heavy, just like me and Heather (my sister),
O rcas and otters, they live in the ocean,
M inecraft and maths, one makes me mad, the other makes me mischievous,
A nimals are awesome, some eat apples, some are angry,
S ausages are sizzling, scrumptious as always.

Thomas Maddison (10)
Willington School, Wimbledon

This Is Me

R acing cars are my favourite
O utdoors is where I like to be
R acing my bike is the best thing of all
Y es, believe me, I will be a Tour rider!

B ouldering and climbing are a great challenge
U nder the water, I love swimming
S kiing on black runs is the best
H umorous is what I often am.

Rory Bush (7)
Willington School, Wimbledon

A Recipe For Me

First, gather gaming and fun
Stir in a cauldron of bravery and immense leadership
Season with a hurricane of rugby and climbing
Add a pinch of family and kindness
Pour in an overflowing waterfall of sleeping and TV
Add an overgrowing mountain of climbing and meat
Blend eating, friends, creativeness
Then, warm happily, and buy it a pet.

James Douglas (10)
Willington School, Wimbledon

Tom's Recipe

This is my recipe...
You need:
10 grams of kindness,
1.5 chunks of nice-looking face,
3 teaspoons of hugs,
1 black Labrador,
1.9 grams of loudness,
5 small spoons of homework,
1 big spoon of school,
A bunch of flowers and some chocolate,
100 tablespoons of smiles,
Stir in some fizzy water,
And this is me!

Tom Parry (7)
Willington School, Wimbledon

My Universe, My World

First, gather my Nintendo and Prime
Stir in some delicious junk food and sweets
Season with family, tennis and golf
Add a pinch of smartness and my soul
Pour in a planet's worth of money
And sprinkle some Fortnite with drinking Prime
Blend chugging and eating, gaming and peeping
Then, warm gently, by finishing with sleeping.

Ian Byun (9)
Willington School, Wimbledon

A Recipe For Me

First, gather cheekiness and an ocean of enthusiasm,
Stir in some athleticism and speediness,
Season with books and a hint of gaming,
Add a pinch of tonic water and a few sweets,
Pour in a mountain of sport,
And a meal of kebabs,
Blend in a handful of sleep and a waterful of gum,
Then, warm gently with a family gathering.

Oscar Ahmadi (10)
Willington School, Wimbledon

England, My Home!

E ngland is my cosy home
N othing can be better
G lad I live in Wimbledon, SW19 is the best!
L ove eating pizza, sushi and all the rest
A lways thinking about football, day and night
N ow I am in Year 3, what a delight!
D oing the multiplication race, however, keeps me up all night!

Eshan Sujenthiran (7)
Willington School, Wimbledon

William

W ith pride, I sit on my gaming chair like I am the king.
I n the cricket pitch, I whack the ball for six.
L ying on my bed with pride.
L iving my life in an amazing world.
I n the pool, I race like a fish.
A n amazing shot on the beautiful tennis court.
M y amazing life, I cherish it with love.

William Campbell (10)
Willington School, Wimbledon

A Recipe For Chaos

First, gather creativity and honesty,
Stir in a love for demolition,
Season with kickboxing and putpocketing,
Add a pinch of animal love and smarts,
Pour in Roblox, Fortnite and all games nice,
And Lucozade with lovely food,
Blend dodgeball, basketball and swimming,
Then, warm gently, by snorkelling in Cyprus.

Samuel Reeve (9)
Willington School, Wimbledon

A Recipe For Me, Me And More Me

First, gather football and fun
Stir in amazing adventures and honey
Season with friendliness and friendship
Add a pinch of flying and food
Pour in parties and playing lots of rugby
Add my great golden retriever mixed up with music
Blend brilliance and love with sportiness and sweets
Warm gently with family.

James Lloyd (9)
Willington School, Wimbledon

Amazing Alex

A mazing at swimming and tennis
L aidback at the weekends
E ating bags of crisps joyfully
X enial to everyone I meet
A stonishing classwork
N ever unkind to people
D elightful during lessons
E ager to learn more and more
R esilient in all I do.

Alex Bartocci (10)
Willington School, Wimbledon

A Recipe For Me

First, gather sports and history,
Stir in athletics with running,
Season with gaming on the Xbox,
Add a pinch of outdoor learning,
Pour in a mountain's worth of honesty,
And a mound of funny friends,
Blend castles, dens and explorations,
Then, warm gently by mixing Halloween and reading.

Hudson Walker (9)
Willington School, Wimbledon

A Recipe For Felix!

First, gather iPad and Prime,
Stir in PS5 and wrestling people,
Season with chicken shawarma and Roblox,
Add a pinch of friends and Dr Pepper,
Pour in a Bentley and an ocean of burgers, and whipped cream and fries,
Blend dreams, pets, wrestling,
And warm gently by gathering friends and family.

Felix Bown (9)
Willington School, Wimbledon

This Is Me

I am Elias
I am sporty
I am kind and brave
Funny and full of laughter

If you put me in a mood, you'll regret it
I'll be no more fun, just a body of grumpiness

I love football, cricket and rugby
It's what we do at school
I guess I'm just lucky.

Elias Carle-Edgar (10)
Willington School, Wimbledon

All About Me

I'm a very good footballer,
I'm good at handball,
I like tennis and am good at it,
I love playing Dragon City and Dragon Temple,
I can build a twenty-year-old Lego,
I love to do PE,
I like to go to Spain when it is half term,
I like to play with my friends,
I like to read.

Danny Han (7)
Willington School, Wimbledon

Me, Me And Only Me

First, gather football and money
Stir in a bee's special honey
Season with deep sleeping
Add a pinch of ravenous eating
Pour in FIFA and amazingness
Add a sniff of craziness
Blend a bin and a win, boots and far from the truth
Then, warm gently with Scorpions, my football club.

Perry Davis (9)
Willington School, Wimbledon

All About Me

I am me and my dad is German,
My mum is French and I am English,
I am a sushi eater too!
Superstar at football,
Making all these goals!
Dalmatians are my school team,
And are fluffy like me!
Rabbits go boing boing,
Makes me feel happy,
So they are my favourite animal!

Raphael Balthasar (7)
Willington School, Wimbledon

Tennis

Sam is a boy who loves sports
And is always amazing on court.
On grass or on clay
He plays on it all day.
With his new Wilson racquet
You should see how hard he can smack it.
He hits winners galore
With the crowd asking for more
And his winner can get up to speeds of 104.

Samuel Cryer (10)
Willington School, Wimbledon

The Perfect Recipe

First, gather Fortnite and hyperactivity
Stir in YouTube and wrestling and reading
Season with philosophy and video games
Add a pinch of family and rugby
Pour in football and fun
And gaming and atoms
Blend self-esteem and coolness
Then, warm gently with atheism and resilience.

Charlie Laffey (9)
Willington School, Wimbledon

A Recipe Of What I Love

Start by putting in some freshly caught fish
Then, put in a bit of funniness
A pinch of bravery
After, put in an ocean breeze of books
Blend some hugs in
And grind some love
Then, warm gently with a family reuniting

And, at the very end, season with some tenderness.

Jack Gale (9)
Willington School, Wimbledon

Me, The Only Me

First, gather board games and origami
Stir in a pitch of rugby
Season with a handful of sweets
Add a pinch of arts and crafts
Pour in a jug of creativity
Add a sprinkle of cheek and silliness
Blend in adventures and walks

Then, warm gently by telling piles of jokes.

Edgar Favre (9)
Willington School, Wimbledon

Joseph Recipe!

First, gather Prime and electronics,
Stir in Robux and aeroplanes.
Season with Dr Pepper and ketchup
Add a pinch of philosophy
Pour in oceans of burgers and love.
Add hot dogs and rugby.
Blend in TV and honesty
And, last but not least, a sweetening Oreo milkshake.

Joseph Benjamin (9)
Willington School, Wimbledon

Ice Cream

I like cold and sweet things
C hocolate also inside
E veryone likes it

C herry topping is on the top
R ussian also likes it
E at! But just one a day
A re you curious? Okay
M y favourite thing is ice cream.

Amy Choi (7)
Willington School, Wimbledon

Recipe For Me

First, gather friendliness and fun.
Stir in a box of exciting books.
Season with cycling and sleeping.
Add in a pinch of funny friends.
Pour in a mountain of wisdom
And a stream of grumpiness.
Blend in culture, tradition and language.
Then, warm with family.

Aaron Li (9)
Willington School, Wimbledon

My Life

First, gather plants and flowers.
Stir in stickers and bunnies and sleepiness.
Season with soup and salmon sushi.
Add a pinch of water thoroughly.
Pour in a lake of lasagne and family.
Blend food and dinner and dyslexia.

Then, warm gently with the school.

Alexander Harvie (9)
Willington School, Wimbledon

Me, Me, Me

Me, me, me
What can I be
Sitting on the tree
Dreaming of future me?

Can I be Elvis?
Rocking my pelvis?
Can I dribble like Kobe?
Or move like Obi-Wan Kenobi?

I am free
I am me
And most importantly

I am Benji.

Benji Hutton (10)
Willington School, Wimbledon

George

G ood football fan and player as well
E ndangering rugby, I sometimes play
O ver the mountain, cycling I go
R ocking guitar music all around
G ood friend, kind mostly, but angry at times
E specially good at tennis!

George Hanna (7)
Willington School, Wimbledon

I Am Unique

A lways friendly and helpful
E ver so beautiful
M ostly smiling and happy
E motionally intelligent
L oving to everyone
I mmensely selfless and kind
A lways fair to my parents - with a mischievous side!

Aemelia Flook (7)
Willington School, Wimbledon

Upset Dog

I am sad,
You took the *ball*, this makes me mad.
I will melt into a pile of fluff
You took the thing I love, that's rough.
I thought we were having fun, now I'm melancholy
Give me my *ball*, then I'll be jolly.

Eddie Rossmann
Willington School, Wimbledon

Me, Myself And I

M yself, how I love myself.
Y our love, how I love your love.
S eeing the football match, how I love the football matches.
E xercise, how I love exercise.
L oot, how I love loot
F ood, how I love food.

Adam Radwan (10)
Willington School, Wimbledon

I Am Me

I am imaginative
I am an energetic kid
My favourite animal is a Komodo dragon
And I really like golden retrievers
I love Pokémon, I like Charizard best
I like being by water, it makes me feel calm
I am happy being me.

Christian Stephenson (8)
Willington School, Wimbledon

This Is Me!

I am Albert Einstein in a school uniform;
I am Pythagoras for the modern days.
I am as kind as Buddah in the living form;
I also like going on planes.
My hair is coal,
And my eyes are brown marbles.

This is me.

Seojun Kim (10)
Willington School, Wimbledon

Heather's Recipe

A bucket of imagination,
Stir in obedience,
Sprinkle in some silence,
And a dash of plain old luck,
2 spoonfuls of kindness,
And a whole bedroom full of honesty,
Mix it up together,
And there you have a Heather.

Heather Maddison (7)
Willington School, Wimbledon

Gio's Cook Book

A spoon of sun makes me red,
A cup of sandcastle makes me yellow,
A bowl of tennis makes me green,
A mug of fruits makes me orange,
A handful of Black Panther makes me violet,
A scoop of rain makes me blue,
Who am I?

Gio Lee (7)
Willington School, Wimbledon

All About Me

A lfie is what everyone calls me
L eopards are my favourite big cat
F riends say I am fast
R eading gets my imagination working
E ach of my siblings are funny
D anson is my surname.

Alfie Danson (7)
Willington School, Wimbledon

Oscar's Favourite Myths

- **O** litau is a big forest
- **S** cary super-sized bat
- **C** erberus, fierce three-headed dog
- **A** nubis, jackal-headed god,
- **R** oc is an enormous elephant-eating bird

All are my happiest dreams.

Oscar Caceres (7)
Willington School, Wimbledon

Noah K B

N oah is always up for a challenge.
O bviously amazing.
A mazing football ability.
H appy except when asked to do work.

K ing of basketball.

B ad like the Barbie.

Noah Kingsley-Benjamin (10)
Willington School, Wimbledon

Fantastic Me

S uper amazing at all sorts of sports and handsome
O verpowered and clever I am
N ever give up is what I do
N o racism or sexism allowed
Y o-yo I am because I spin in different ways.

Sonny Browne (10)
Willington School, Wimbledon

The Thing I Most Like

I am a goalkeeper,
And I don't like a weeper,
I do like cooking,
And definitely looking
At planes
And trains,
I like boats
And goats,
But the thing I like most
Is riding my bike.

Alfie Harper (7)
Willington School, Wimbledon

Calum's Acrostic Poem

C alum is an Iron Bru drinker
A TV for myself is the best
L ove to be an astonishing goalkeeper
U nbelievably clever at maths
M aking cakes is my favourite hobby.

Calum Stimpson (7)
Willington School, Wimbledon

This Is Me

I am fun,
I am mischievous,
I can do anything!
I love basketball,
I have great friends,
I love learning and playing the violin,
All these things make me who I am,
I am Jasper!

Jasper Cristina (8)
Willington School, Wimbledon

All About Me

A yoon is my name
Y ellow is my favourite colour
O range is my favourite fruit
O cean sand makes me fresh
N ice things make me happy.

Ayoon Jeong (7)
Willington School, Wimbledon

Vasil's Riddle

My animal has two legs,
Has wings but cannot fly,
It lives in Antarctica,
It does not have a lot of fur,
What is my animal?

Answer: A penguin

Vasil Vasilev
Willington School, Wimbledon

How To Make Me

3 footballs,
My family,
My home,
My dog,
Books,
My dad,
My mum,
A dash of kindness.

Joe Blythe (7)
Willington School, Wimbledon

Amazing Me

L evitatingly lucky
U nforgettably kind
C an do anything
A mazingly handsome.

Luca Broere (11)
Willington School, Wimbledon

I Am Julian Paul

I love Dragon City,
Julian Paul is my name,
Alfie's real name is Alfred,
Noah is my best friend.

Julian Paul (7)
Willington School, Wimbledon

YoungWriters
Est. 1991

YOUNG WRITERS INFORMATION

We hope you have enjoyed reading this book – and that you will continue to in the coming years.

If you're the parent or family member of an enthusiastic poet or story writer, do visit our website **www.youngwriters.co.uk/subscribe** and sign up to receive news, competitions, writing challenges and tips, activities and much, much more! There's lots to keep budding writers motivated!

If you would like to order further copies of this book, or any of our other titles, then please give us a call or order via your online account.

Young Writers
Remus House
Coltsfoot Drive
Peterborough
PE2 9BF
(01733) 890066
info@youngwriters.co.uk

Join in the conversation!
Tips, news, giveaways and much more!

YoungWritersUK YoungWritersCW youngwriterscw

Scan me to watch the This Is Me video!